MW00855981

Sola Scriptura

An Orthodox Analysis of the Cornerstone of Reformation Theology

By Fr. John Whiteford

PREFACE

This booklet is intended primarily to assist Orthodox Christians in understanding the Protestant doctrine of *sola Scriptura,* so that they can discuss this aspect of theology intelligently with Protestants. However, Protestants who are seeking to understand the Orthodox approach to the interpretation and use of Scripture will also find this booklet helpful.

CONTENTS

Introduction

WHY SCRIPTURE ALONE? 5

Section I

PROBLEMS WITH THE DOCTRINE OF SOLA SCRIPTURA 9

A. IT IS BASED ON FALSE ASSUMPTIONS 9
FALSE ASSUMPTION # 1:
The Bible was intended to be the final word on faith, piety, and worship . . 10
a) Do the Scriptures themselves teach that they are "all sufficient"? 10
b) What was the purpose of the New Testament writings? 12
c) Is the Bible, in practice, really "all sufficient" for Protestants?....... 15
FALSE ASSUMPTION # 2:
The Scriptures were the basis of the early Church, whereas Tradition
is simply a human corruption that came much later 16
FALSE ASSUMPTION # 3:
Christians can interpret the Scriptures for themselves, without the
aid of the Church 21

B. THE DOCTRINE OF SOLA SCRIPTURA DOES NOT
MEET ITS OWN CRITERIA 23

C. PROTESTANT INTERPRETIVE APPROACHES THAT
DON'T WORK.. 23
APPROACH # 1: Just take the Bible literally—the meaning is clear 25
APPROACH # 2: The Holy Spirit provides the correct understanding ... 25
APPROACH # 3: Let the clear passages interpret the unclear 26
APPROACH # 4: Historical-critical exegesis 27

Section II

THE ORTHODOX APPROACH TO HOLY SCRIPTURE.......... 34
"EVERYWHERE"... 39
"ALWAYS" 41
"AND BY ALL" 42

CONCLUSION.. 43
APPENDIX: Empiricist Assumptions in Protestant Scholarship 46

ACKNOWLEDGEMENTS

I would like to express my gratitude to His Grace, Bishop Hilarion of Washington, D.C. (Russian Orthodox Church Abroad) who has given me his blessing to have this work published. I must also express my indebtedness to Father Anthony Nelson and the faithful of St. Benedict's Orthodox Church in Oklahoma City, who introduced my wife and me to the Faith; to Mrs. Anastasia Titov, who was St. John Maximovitch's secretary in Shanghai, and whose depth of wisdom and Orthodox piety have been an inspiration; to Frank Schaeffer for publishing the original version of this work in *The Christian Activist;* and finally to my wife, Matushka Patricia, for her patience, love, and support throughout our pilgrimage to Orthodoxy, as well as in our struggle to live out the Faith.

—Deacon John Whiteford

Introduction

WHY SCRIPTURE ALONE?

S ince my conversion from evangelical Protestantism to Orthodox Christianity, I have noted a general amazement among many of those who have been raised Orthodox that a Protestant could be converted. This is not because the Orthodox are uncertain about their own faith. Usually they are just amazed that anything could break through a Protestant's mysteriously "stubborn" insistence on being wrong!

What I have come to understand is that most Orthodox people have a confused and limited grasp of what Protestantism is, and what its adherents believe. Thus when "cradle Orthodox" believers have encounters with Protestants, even though they both may use the same words, they do not generally communicate because they do not speak the same theological language. In other words, they have very little common theological basis from which to discuss their differences. Of course when one considers that some twenty thousand-plus different Protestant groups now exist (with only the one common trait, that each group claims to rightly understand the Bible), one must certainly sympathize with those who are a bit confused by all of this.

Protestants in search of theological sanity, of true worship, and of the ancient Christian Faith are practically beating on the doors of the Orthodox Church. They are no longer satisfied with the contradictions and the faddishness of contemporary Protestant America. But when we Orthodox open the door to these inquirers we must be prepared: these people have questions! Many of these inquirers are Protestant ministers, or are among the better-informed laymen. They are sincere seekers of Truth, but they have much to unlearn and it will require informed Orthodox Christians to help them work through these issues. Orthodox Christians must understand Protestants' basic assumptions, but even more importantly, they must know what they believe themselves!

While understanding his own Faith is the first and most basic requirement for one who would communicate the Faith to the non-Orthodox, we must also learn how to communicate that Faith in a way which will be understood by them. In order successfully to communicate the Orthodox Faith to Protestants, we must equip ourselves with sufficient knowledge and understanding of their beliefs, and where we differ. To understand the unique beliefs of each individual Protestant group requires a knowledge of the history and development of Protestantism in general, a great deal of research into each major branch of Protestant theology and worship, and a measure of contemporary reading in order to understand some of the more important cross-trends that are currently at work (such as liberalism, or emotionalism). Even with all this, one could not hope to keep up with the new groups that spring up almost daily. I can't, and I was a Protestant myself! Yet, for all their differences, there is one basic underlying assumption that unites these disparate groups into the general category of "Protestant."

Essentially all Protestant denominations believe that they rightly understand the Bible. And though they may disagree on what the Bible says, they generally do agree on how one is to interpret the Bible: on one's own, apart from Church Tradition.[1] If one can come to understand this belief, why it is wrong, and how one is rightly to

---

[1] Some Protestant traditions do claim to use Tradition to one degree or another, but unfortunately it is generally given only lip service. In most cases, Tradition is only called upon when it supports a view that a given Protestant wishes to buttress. For example, one will often hear evangelicals speak of the "historic Christian Faith" when debating with those they consider "cultists," particularly when defending the doctrine of the Trinity. But when confronted with an aspect of the historic Christian Faith that they do not agree with, these same apologists will dismiss Holy Tradition with just as quick a wave of the hands as do Mormons and Jehovah's Witnesses.

approach the Holy Scriptures, then one can engage any Protestant of any denomination in a discussion of Orthodox Christianity with understanding.

Even groups as different as the Baptists and the Jehovah's Witnesses are really not as different as they outwardly appear, once you have understood this essential point. Indeed, if you ever have an opportunity to watch a Baptist and a Jehovah's Witness argue over the Bible, you will notice that in the final analysis they simply quote different scriptures back and forth at each other. If they are equally matched intellectually, neither will get anywhere in the discussion, because they both essentially agree on their approach to the Bible. And because neither questions their common underlying assumption, neither can see that their mutually flawed approach to the Scriptures is the real problem.

Now in saying that Jehovah's Witnesses approach the Scriptures in essentially the same way as do most evangelicals or fundamentalists, am I suggesting that there is no difference between them? Not at all! In fact, that is precisely the point. There is a world of difference between the average Southern Baptist, who believes in the Trinity, and a Jehovah's Witness who does not. No one would ever accuse the Orthodox of demeaning the importance of the doctrine of the Trinity! The point is, since Baptists and Jehovah's Witnesses share a common approach to the Scriptures and yet come to such drastically different conclusions on this essential doctrine, obviously, something is wrong with the approach.

WHY SCRIPTURE ALONE?

If we are to understand what Protestants think, we will first have to know why they believe what they believe. In fact, if we try to put ourselves in the place of early reformers such as Martin Luther, we must certainly have some appreciation for their reasons for championing the doctrine of *sola Scriptura* (or "Scripture alone"). When one considers the corruption in the Roman Church at that time, the degenerate teachings it promoted, and the distorted understanding of Tradition that it used to defend itself—along with the fact that the West was several centuries removed from any significant contact with its former Orthodox heritage—it is difficult to imagine within those limitations how one such as Luther might have responded with significantly better results. How could Luther have appealed to Tradition to fight these abuses, when Tradition (as all in the Roman West had been led to believe) was embodied in the very papacy that was responsible for those abuses? To Luther, it was Tradition that had erred. And if he were to reform the Church, he would have to do so with the sure undergirding of the Scriptures.

However, Luther never really sought to eliminate Tradition altogether, and he certainly did not use the Scriptures truly "alone." What he really attempted to do was to use Scripture to get rid of those parts of the Roman tradition that were corrupt. Unfortunately, his rhetoric far outstripped his own practice, and more radical reformers took the idea of *sola Scriptura* to its logical conclusion.

Section I

PROBLEMS WITH THE DOCTRINE OF SOLA SCRIPTURA

A. IT IS BASED ON FALSE ASSUMPTIONS

An assumption is something that we take for granted from the outset, usually quite unconsciously. As long as an assumption is a true and valid one, all is well. But a false assumption obviously leads to false conclusions. One would hope that even when someone has made an unconscious assumption, if his conclusions are proven faulty, he would then ask himself where his underlying error lay.

Protestants who are willing honestly to assess the current state of the Protestant world, for instance, must ask themselves, "If Protestantism's foundational teaching of *sola Scriptura* is of God, why has it resulted in the formation of over twenty thousand differing groups that can't agree on basic aspects of what the Bible says, or even on what it means to be a Christian? If the Bible is sufficient apart from Holy Tradition, why can a Baptist, a charismatic, a Methodist, and even a Jehovah's Witness all claim to believe what the Bible says, and yet no two of them agree on what it is that the Bible says?"

Clearly, here is a situation in which Protestants find themselves, which is without a doubt at odds with the Church we find in the New Testament. Unfortunately, most Protestants are willing to blame this sad state of affairs on almost anything except the true root problem.

Mind you, the problem here is not the integrity of the Bible. The Bible is inspired by the Holy Spirit, and is received by the Church as the Word of God. We are not arguing here the inspiration of Scripture, but rather its proper use.

The idea of *sola Scriptura* is so foundational to Protestantism, to them it is tantamount to denying God even to question it. But as our Lord said, "Every good tree bringeth forth good fruit; but a bad tree bringeth forth evil fruit" (Matthew 7:17). If we judge *sola Scriptura* by its fruit, then we are left with no other conclusion than that this tree needs to be "hewn down, and cast into the fire" (Matthew 7:19).

FALSE ASSUMPTION #1: The Bible was intended to be the final word on faith, piety, and worship.

a) Do the Scriptures themselves teach that they are "all sufficient" apart from Church Tradition?

The most obvious assumption that underlies the doctrine of "Scripture alone" is that the Bible has within it all that is needed for the Christian life—for true faith, practice, piety, and worship. The passage that is most often cited to support this notion is:

> . . . from a child thou hast known the Holy Scriptures, which are able to make thee wise unto salvation through faith which is in Christ Jesus. All scripture is given by inspiration of God, and is profitable for doctrine, for reproof, for correction, for instruction in righteousness: that the man of God may be perfect, thoroughly furnished unto all good works (2 Timothy 3:15-17).

Those who would use these verses to advocate *sola Scriptura* argue that this passage teaches the "all sufficiency" of Scripture—because, "If, indeed, the Holy Scriptures are able to make the pious man perfect . . . then, indeed to attain completeness and perfection, there is no need of tradition." [2] But is this really what this passage teaches?

---

[2] George Mastrantonis, trans., *Augsburg and Constantinople: The Correspondence between the Tubingen Theologians and Patriarch Jeremiah II of Constantinople on the Augsburg Confession* (Brookline, MA: Holy Cross Orthodox Press, 1982), p. 114.

To begin with, we should ask what the Apostle Paul is talking about when he speaks of the "Holy Scriptures" Saint Timothy has known since he was a child. We can be sure that Saint Paul is not referring to the New Testament, because the New Testament had not yet been written when Saint Timothy was a child. In fact, only a few of the books of the New Testament had been written when Saint Paul wrote this epistle to Saint Timothy. They certainly had not been collected together into the canon of the New Testament as we know it today.

Obviously here, and in most references to the Scriptures that we find in the New Testament, Saint Paul is speaking of the Old Testament. Therefore, if this passage is going to be used to set the limits on inspired authority, not only will Tradition be excluded, but this passage itself—and the entire New Testament!

In the second place, if Saint Paul meant here to exclude Tradition as not being profitable, then we should wonder why he uses non-biblical oral tradition in this very same chapter. The names Jannes and Jambres are not found in the Old Testament, yet in 2 Timothy 3:8 Saint Paul refers to them as opposing Moses.

The Apostle Paul is drawing here upon the oral tradition that the names of the two most prominent Egyptian magicians in the Exodus account (chapters 7; 8) were "Jannes" and "Jambres."[3] And this is by no means the only time a nonbiblical source is used in the New Testament. The best-known instance is in the Epistle of Saint Jude, which quotes from the Book of Enoch (Jude 14, 15; cf. Enoch 1:9).

The primary purpose in the Church establishing an authoritative list of books which were to be received as sacred Scripture was to protect the Church from spurious books which claimed apostolic authorship, but were in fact the work of heretics, such as the "Gospel of Thomas." Heretical groups could not base their teachings on Holy

---

[3] A. F. Walls, "Jannes and Jambres," *The Illustrated Bible Dictionary,* vol. 2 (Wheaton, IL: Tyndale House Publishers, 1980), pp. 733-734.

Tradition because their teachings originated from outside the Church. So the only way they could claim any authoritative basis for their heresies was to twist the meaning of the Scriptures and to forge new books in the names of Apostles or Old Testament saints.

In establishing an authoritative list of sacred books that were received by all as being divinely inspired and of genuine Old Testament or apostolic origin, the Church did not intend to imply that all of the Christian Faith and all information necessary for worship and good order in the Church was contained in these writings.[4] In fact, by the time the Church settled the canon of Scripture, it was already, in its faith and worship, essentially indistinguishable from the Church of later periods. This is an historical certainty. As for the structure of Church authority, it was Orthodox bishops, gathered together in various councils, who settled the question of the canon. The Church as we know it was in place *before* the Bible as we know it was in place.

b) What was the purpose of the New Testament writings?

In Protestant biblical studies, it is taught (and I think correctly) that when studying the Bible, among many other considerations, one must consider the genre (or literary type) of a particular passage: different genres have different uses. Another consideration is, of course, the subject and purpose of the book or passage.

In the New Testament we have, broadly speaking, four literary genres: Gospel, historical narrative (Acts), epistle, and apocalyptic/prophetic writing (Revelation). The Gospels were written to testify of Christ's Incarnation, life, death, and Resurrection. Biblical

---

[4] Indeed this list did not even intend to comprise all the books which the Church has preserved from antiquity and considers part of the larger Tradition. For example, the Book of Enoch, though quoted in the canonical books, was not itself included in the canon. I will not pretend to know why this is so, but for whatever reasons the Church has chosen to preserve this book, and yet has not appointed it to be read in Church or to be set alongside the canonical books.

historical narratives recount the history of God's people and also the lives of significant figures in that history, and show God's providence in the midst of it all. Epistles were written primarily to answer specific problems that arose in various churches; thus, things that were assumed and understood by all, and not considered problems, were not generally addressed in any detail. Doctrinal issues that were addressed were generally disputed or misunderstood doctrines.[5] Matters of worship were only dealt with when there were related problems (for example, 1 Corinthians 11—14). Apocalyptic writings, such as Revelation, were written to show God's ultimate triumph in history.

Interestingly, none of these literary types present in the New Testament has worship as a primary subject, nor was any of them meant to give details about how to worship in church. In the Old Testament there are detailed, though by no means exhaustive, treatments of the worship of Israel (Exodus, Leviticus, and Psalms). In the New Testament, there are only the meagerest hints of the worship of the early Christians. Why is this? Certainly not because they had no order in their services—liturgical historians have established the fact that early Christians continued to worship in a manner firmly based upon the patterns of Jewish worship, which they inherited from the Apostles.[6]

However, even the few references in the New Testament that touch upon the worship of the early Church show that New Testament Christians worshiped liturgically, as did their fathers before

---

[5] For example, there is no place where the question of the inerrancy of the Scriptures is dealt with in detail, precisely because this was not an issue of dispute. In our present day, with the rise of religious skepticism, this is very much an issue, and if the epistles were being written today, this would certainly be dealt with at some point. It would thus be foolish to conclude that since this issue is not dealt with specifically, that the early Christians did not think it was important or did not believe in it.

[6] Alexander Schmemann, *Introduction to Liturgical Theology* (Crestwood, NY: St. Vladimir's Seminary Press, 1986), pp. 51ff.

them: they observed hours of prayer (Acts 3:1); they worshiped in the temple (Acts 2:46; 3:1; 21:26); and they worshiped in synagogues (Acts 18:4).

We also need to note that none of the types of literature present in the New Testament has as its purpose comprehensive doctrinal instruction. The New Testament contains neither a catechism nor a systematic theology. If all we need as Christians is the Bible by itself, why does it not contain some sort of comprehensive doctrinal statement? Imagine how easily all the many controversies could have been settled if the Bible had clearly answered every doctrinal question. But as convenient as it might have been, such things are not found among the books of the Bible.

Let no one misunderstand the point that is being made. None of this is meant to belittle the importance of the Holy Scriptures. God forbid! In the Orthodox Church the Scriptures are believed to be fully inspired, inerrant, and authoritative. But the fact is that the Bible does not contain teaching on every subject of importance to the Church.

As already stated, the New Testament gives little detail about how to worship—and this is certainly no small matter. Furthermore, the same Church that handed down to us the Holy Scriptures, and preserved them, was the very Church from which we have received our patterns of worship! If we mistrust this Church's faithfulness in preserving apostolic worship, then we must also mistrust her fidelity in preserving the Scriptures.[7]

---

[7] And in fact, this is what Protestant scholarship has done. Though Protestantism was founded on its claim of believing the Bible to be the only authority for faith and practice, contemporary Protestant scholarship is dominated by modernists who no longer believe in the inspiration or inerrancy of the Scriptures. They now place themselves above the Bible and only choose to use those parts that suit them, discarding the rest as "primitive mythology and legend." The only authority left for such as these is themselves.

c) Is the Bible, in practice, really "all sufficient" for Protestants?

Protestants frequently claim they "just believe the Bible," but a number of questions arise when one examines their actual use of the Bible. For instance, why do Protestants write so many books on doctrine and the Christian life in general, if indeed all that is necessary is the Bible? If the Bible by itself were sufficient for one to understand it, then why don't Protestants simply hand out Bibles and let it go at that? And if it is "all sufficient," as they suggest, why do Protestants not all believe the same?

What is the purpose of Sunday school, or the many Protestant study Bibles, if all that is needed is the Bible itself? Why do they hand out tracts and other material? Why do they even teach or preach at all—why not just read the Bible to people? Though they usually will not admit it, they instinctively know the Bible cannot be understood alone. And in fact, every Protestant sect has its own body of traditions, though again they generally will not call them by this name.

It is not an accident that Orthodox Presbyterians all believe the same things, and United Pentecostals generally believe the same things, but Orthodox Presbyterians and United Pentecostals emphatically do not believe the same things. Orthodox Presbyterians and United Pentecostals do not each individually come up with their own ideas from an independent study of the Bible. Rather, those in each group are all taught to believe in a certain way—from a common tradition.

Thus, the question is not really whether we will just believe the Bible or whether we will also use tradition. The real question is, *which* tradition will we use to interpret the Bible? Which tradition can be trusted—the Apostolic Tradition of the historic Church, or the modern and divergent traditions of Protestantism, which have no roots deeper than the advent of the Protestant Reformation?

FALSE ASSUMPTION #2: The Scriptures were the basis of the early Church, whereas Tradition is simply a human corruption that came much later.

Especially among today's evangelicals and charismatics, you will find the word "tradition" is a derogatory term. To label something as a "tradition" is roughly equivalent to saying it is "fleshly," "spiritually dead," "destructive," or "legalistic." As Protestants read the New Testament, it seems clear to them that the Bible always condemns tradition as being opposed to Scripture. The assumption is that the early Christians were pretty much like today's evangelicals or charismatics, but with beards and togas. That the first-century Christians would have had liturgical worship, or bishops, or would have adhered to any tradition at all, is inconceivable. Only later, "when the Church became corrupted," is it imagined that such things entered the Church.

It comes as quite a blow to such Protestants (as it did to me) when they actually study the early Church and the writings of the early Fathers and begin to see a distinctly different picture from that which they were led to envision. One finds, for example, the early Christians did not tote their Bibles with them to church each Sunday. It was so difficult to acquire a copy of even portions of Scripture, due to the time and resources involved in making a copy, that very few individuals owned their own copies. Instead, the copies of the Scriptures were kept by designated persons in the church, or kept at the place where the church gathered for worship (in which context the Scriptures were read corporately).

Furthermore, most churches did not have complete copies of all the books even of the Old Testament, much less the New Testament—which was not completed until the end of the first century, and not in its final canonical form until the fourth century. This is not to say the early Christians did not study the Scriptures—they did, in earnest, but as a group, not as individuals. And for most of the first century, Christians were limited in their study of the Scriptures to the Old Testament.

So how did they know the truth of the Gospel, the life and teachings of Christ, how to worship, what to believe about the Person and natures of Christ? They had the Tradition handed down from the Apostles.

Sure, many in the early Church heard these things directly from the Apostles themselves, but many more did not. Later generations had access to the writings of the Apostles through the New Testament, but the early Church depended almost entirely on oral and liturgical tradition for its knowledge of the Christian Faith.

This dependence upon Tradition is evident in the New Testament writings themselves. For example, Saint Paul exhorts the Thessalonians: "Therefore, brethren, stand fast and hold the traditions which ye have been taught, whether by word [oral tradition] or our epistle" (2 Thessalonians 2:15).

The word here translated "traditions" is the Greek word *paradosis*. The word itself literally means "that which is transmitted, or delivered." It is the same word used when referring negatively to the false traditions of the Pharisees (Mark 7:3, 5, 8), and also when referring to authoritative Christian teaching (1 Corinthians 11:2; 2 Thessalonians 2:15).

So what makes the tradition of the Pharisees false and that of the Church true? The source!

Christ made clear what was the source of the traditions of the Pharisees when He called them "the traditions of men" (Mark 7:8). Saint Paul, on the other hand, in reference to Christian Tradition, states, "I praise you brethren, that you remember me in all things and hold fast to the traditions [*paradoseis*] just as I delivered [*paredoka*, a verbal form of *paradosis*] them to you" (1 Corinthians 11:2). And where did Saint Paul get these traditions in the first place? "I received from the Lord that which I delivered [*paredoka*] to you" (1 Corinthians 11:23).

What the Orthodox Church refers to when it speaks of the Apostolic Tradition is "the Faith once delivered [*paradotheise*] unto the saints" (Jude 3). Its source is Christ, and it was delivered personally by Him to the Apostles through all that He said and did—which, if it all were written down, "the world itself could not contain the books that should be written" (John 21:25). The Apostles in turn delivered this Tradition to the entire Church. And the Church, being the repository of this treasure, thus became "the pillar and ground of the Truth" (1 Timothy 3:15).

The testimony of the New Testament is clear on this point: the early Christians had both oral and written traditions which they received from Christ through the Apostles. For written tradition they at first had only portions—one local church had an epistle, another perhaps a Gospel. Gradually these writings were gathered together into collections, and ultimately, under the guidance of the Holy Spirit in the Church, they became the New Testament. And how did these early Christians know which books were authentic and which were not—for (as already noted) there were numerous spurious epistles and gospels claimed by heretics to have been written by Apostles? It was the Apostolic Tradition that aided the Church in making this determination.

Protestants react violently to the idea of Holy Tradition simply because the only form of it they have generally encountered is the distorted concept of tradition found in Roman Catholicism. Contrary to the Roman view of tradition—which is personified by the Pope, and develops new dogmas without apostolic foundation, such as papal infallibility—the Orthodox do not believe Tradition changes or "develops."

Certainly when the Church is faced with a heresy, it may be forced to define more precisely the difference between truth and error; but the Truth is never altered. It may be said that Tradition expands or matures, but only in the sense that as the Church moves through history, it does not forget its experiences along the way. It remembers the saints that arise in it, and it preserves the writings of those who have accurately stated its faith. But the Faith itself

18

was "once delivered unto the saints" (Jude 3).

How can we know the Church has preserved the Apostolic Tradition in its purity? The short answer is that God has preserved it in the Church because He promised to do so. Christ said that He would build His Church and the gates of hell would not prevail against it (Matthew 16:18). Christ Himself is the Head of the Church (Ephesians 4:15, 16), the Church is His Body (Ephesians 1:22, 23), and He has promised to be with the Church "even unto the end of the world" (Matthew 28:20). Christ did not promise His Church would always be prosperous, or the most numerous of religions; in fact, He promised quite the opposite (Matthew 7:13, 14; 10:22; John 15:20). Neither did Christ promise there would be no sinners in the Church (Matthew 13:47-50), or that it would not have to contend with false shepherds or wolves in sheep's clothing (John 10:1, 12, 13). But Christ did promise an abiding and ultimately triumphant Church, which would have His abiding presence, and would be guided into all Truth by the Holy Spirit (John 16:13). Were the Church to lose the purity of the Apostolic Tradition, then the Truth would have to cease being the Truth—for the Church is the pillar and foundation of the Truth (1 Timothy 3:15).

The common Protestant conception of Church history—that the Church fell into apostasy from the time of Constantine until the Reformation—certainly makes these and many other scriptures meaningless. If the Church had ceased to be for even one day, then the gates of hell would have prevailed against it on that day. If this were the case, when Christ described the growth of the Church in His parable of the mustard seed (Matthew 13:31, 32), He should have spoken of a plant that started to grow but was squashed, and in its place a new seed sprouted later on. Instead, He used the imagery of a mustard seed that begins small, but steadily grows into the largest of garden plants.

As to those who would posit that there was some group of true-believing Protestants living in caves somewhere for a thousand years, where is the evidence for such a group's existence? The Waldensians,[8] who are claimed as ancestors by every sect from the Pentecostals to the Jehovah's Witnesses, did not exist prior to the twelfth century. It is, to say the least, a bit of a stretch to believe that these true-believers suffered courageously under the fierce persecutions of the Romans, and yet would have headed for the hills as soon as Christianity became a legal religion. Yet even this seems possible when compared with the notion that such a group could have survived for a thousand years without leaving a trace of historical evidence to substantiate that it had ever existed.

At this point one might object that there were in fact examples of people in Church history who taught things contrary to what others taught, so who is to say what the Apostolic Tradition is? And furthermore, if a corrupt practice arose, how could it later be distinguished from Apostolic Tradition?

Protestants ask these questions because in the Roman Catholic Church, there did arise new and corrupt traditions. But this happened because the Latin West first altered its understanding of the nature of Tradition.

The Orthodox understanding, which had earlier prevailed in the West and which was preserved in the Orthodox Church, is basically that Tradition is in essence unchanging and is known by

---

[8] The Waldensians were a sect founded in the 12th century by Peter Waldo which in some ways anticipated the Protestant Reformation. Due to persecution by the Roman Catholic Church, this sect survived primarily in the mountainous regions of northwestern Italy. With the advent of the Protestant Reformation, the Waldensians came under the influence of the Reformed movement and essentially joined forces with it. Many early Protestant historians claimed that the Waldensians represented a remnant of "true" Christians that had existed prior to Constantine. Though today no credible historian would make such an unsubstantiated claim, many fundamentalists and cults like the Jehovah's Witnesses continue to claim descent from the early Church through the Waldensians—despite the fact that the Waldensians still exist to this day, and they certainly do not claim the Jehovah's Witnesses.

its universality, or catholicity. True Apostolic Tradition is found in the historic consensus of Church teaching. Find that which the Church has believed always, throughout history, and everywhere, and you will have found the Truth. If any belief can be shown not to have been received by the Church in its history, then this is heresy.

Mind you, however, we are speaking of the Church, not schismatic groups. There were schismatics and heretics that broke away from the Church during the New Testament period, and there has been a continual supply of them since. For as the Apostle says, "there must be also heresies among you, that they which are approved may be made manifest" (1 Corinthians 11:19).

FALSE ASSUMPTION #3: Christians can interpret the Scriptures for themselves, without the aid of the Church.

Though some Protestants might take issue with the way this assumption is worded, this is essentially the belief that prevailed when the Reformers first advocated the doctrine of *sola Scriptura*. The line of reasoning was that the meaning of Scripture is clear enough that anyone could understand it by simply reading it for himself, and thus the Church's help is superfluous.

This position is clearly stated by the Tubingen Lutheran Scholars, who exchanged letters with Patriarch Jeremias II of Constantinople about thirty years after Luther's death:

> Perhaps, someone will say that on the one hand, the Scriptures are absolutely free from error; but on the other hand, they have been concealed by much obscurity, so that without the interpretations of the Spirit-bearing Fathers they could not be clearly understood. But meanwhile this, too, is very true that what has been said in a scarcely perceptible manner in some places in the Scriptures, these same things have been stated in another place in them

explicitly and most clearly so that even the most simple person can understand them.[9]

Though these Lutheran scholars claimed to use the writings of the Holy Fathers, they argued that these writings were unnecessary, and that, where they believed the Scriptures and the Holy Fathers conflicted, the Fathers were to be disregarded.

What they were actually arguing, however, was that when the teachings of the Holy Fathers conflicted with their own private opinions on the Scriptures, their private opinions were to be considered more authoritative than the teachings of the Fathers of the Church. Rather than listening to the Fathers, who had shown themselves righteous and saintly, they gave priority to the human reasonings of the individual. This is the same human reason that has led the most influential Lutheran biblical scholars of the past hundred years to reject many of the essential doctrines of Scripture, and even to reject the inspiration of the Scriptures themselves—the very foundation upon which the early Lutherans claimed to base their entire faith!

In reply, Patriarch Jeremias II clearly exposed the true character of private interpretation:

> Let us accept, then, the traditions of the Church with a sincere heart and not a multitude of rationalizations. For God created man to be upright; instead they sought after diverse ways of rationalizing (Ecclesiastes 7:29). Let us not allow ourselves to learn a new kind of faith which is condemned by the tradition of the Holy Fathers. For the Divine apostle says, "if anyone is preaching to you a Gospel contrary to that which you received, let him be accursed" (Galatians 1:9).[10]

---

[9] Mastrantonis, p. 115.
[10] Mastrantonis, p. 198.

B. THE DOCTRINE OF *SOLA SCRIPTURA* DOES NOT MEET ITS OWN CRITERIA

You might imagine that such a belief system as Protestantism, which has as its cardinal doctrine that Scripture alone is authoritative in matters of faith, would first seek to prove that this cardinal doctrine met its own criteria. One would probably expect Protestants to be able to brandish hundreds of proof-texts from the Scriptures to support this doctrine—upon which all else they believe is based. At the very least, one would hope two or three solid texts which clearly taught this doctrine could be found—since the Scriptures themselves say, "In the mouth of two or three witnesses shall every word be established" (2 Corinthians 13:1).

Yet like the boy in the fable who pointed out that the emperor wore no clothes, I must say there is not one single verse in the entirety of Holy Scripture that teaches the doctrine of *sola Scriptura*. There is not even one that comes close. Oh yes, there are numerous passages in the Bible that speak of its inspiration, of its authority, and of its profitability—but there is no place in the Bible that teaches that Scripture *alone* is authoritative for believers. If such a teaching were even implicit, then surely the early Fathers of the Church would have taught this doctrine also. But which of the Holy Fathers ever taught such a thing? Thus Protestantism's most basic teaching self-destructs, being contrary to itself.

But not only is the Protestant doctrine of *sola Scriptura* not taught in the Scriptures—it is, in fact, specifically contradicted by the Scriptures (which we have already discussed) which teach that Holy Tradition is also binding to Christians (2 Thessalonians 2:15; 1 Corinthians 11:2).

C. PROTESTANT INTERPRETIVE APPROACHES THAT DON'T WORK

Even from the very earliest days of the Reformation, Protestants have been forced to deal with the fact that, just given the Bible and the reasoning power of the individual alone, people could not agree upon the meaning of many of the most basic questions of Christian doctrine. Within Martin Luther's own lifetime dozens of differing groups had already arisen, claiming to "just believe the Bible," but none agreeing with another on what the Bible said. As an example, Luther himself courageously stood before the Diet of Worms with the challenge that, unless he were persuaded by Scripture or by plain reason, he would not retract anything he had been teaching. But later, when the Anabaptists, who disagreed with the Lutherans on a number of points, simply asked for the same indulgence, Lutherans butchered them by the thousands.[11] So much for the rhetoric about the right of the individual to read the Scriptures for himself.

Despite the obvious problems that the rapid splintering of Protestantism presented for the doctrine of *sola Scriptura*, Protestants— not willing to concede defeat to the pope—instead concluded the real problem must be those with whom they disagree. In other words, every other sect but their own must not be reading the Bible correctly. Thus a number of approaches to biblical interpretation have been set forth as solutions to this problem.

Of course, the approach has yet to be invented that could reverse the endless multiplication of schisms. Yet Protestants still search for the elusive methodological "key" that will solve their problem. Let us examine the most popular approaches that have been tried thus far—each still advocated by one group or another.

---

[11] "Although earlier he [Luther] had opposed the burning of Anabaptists by Lutherans, eventually he reluctantly approved the death penalty for them on the grounds that they were guilty of sedition and blasphemy." Kenneth Scott Latourette, *A History of Christianity,* Vol. II: *Reformation to the Present* (New York: Harper & Row, 1975), p. 730, cf. pp. 779f.

See also F. L. Cross and E. A. Livingstone, "Anabaptists," *The Oxford Dictionary of the Christian Church* (Oxford: Oxford University Press, 1974), p. 47.

APPROACH #1: Just take the Bible literally—the meaning is clear.

This approach was without doubt the first approach used by the Reformers, though very early on they came to realize that by itself this was an insufficient solution to the problems presented by the doctrine of *sola Scriptura*. Although this approach was a failure from the start, it is still the most common one to be found among less-educated fundamentalists, evangelicals, and charismatics.

"The Bible says what it means and means what it says," is an oft-heard phrase. But when it comes to scriptural texts that Protestants generally do not agree with—such as when Christ gave the Apostles the power to forgive sins (John 20:23), or when He said of the Eucharist, "This is my body. . . . This is my blood" (Matthew 26:26, 28), or when Paul taught that women should cover their heads in church (1 Corinthians 11:1–16)—then all of a sudden the Bible doesn't say what it means any more. "Why, those verses aren't meant to be taken literally!"

APPROACH #2: The Holy Spirit provides the correct understanding.

Presented with the numerous groups that arose under the banner of the Reformation that could not agree on the interpretation of Scriptures, Protestant scholars next proposed as a solution the assertion that the Holy Spirit would guide pious Protestants to interpret the Scriptures rightly. But everyone who disagreed doctrinally could not possibly be guided by the same Spirit. The result was that each group tended to de-Christianize all those who differed from it.

If this approach were a valid one, we would be left with one group of Protestants which had rightly interpreted the Scriptures. But which one of the thousands of denominations could it be? The answer depends on which Protestant you are speaking to. One thing you can be sure of—those who use this argument invariably are convinced their group is it.

As denominations stacked upon denominations, it became a correspondingly greater stretch for any of them to say with a straight face that only they had it right. So it has become increasingly common to minimize the differences between denominations and simply conclude those differences do not much matter. "Perhaps each group has a piece of the Truth, but none of us has the whole Truth."

APPROACH #3: Let the clear passages interpret the unclear.

This must have seemed the perfect solution to the problem of how to interpret the Bible by itself—let the easily understood passages interpret those which are not clear. The logic of this approach is simple. Though one passage may state a truth obscurely, surely the same truth would be clearly stated elsewhere in Scripture. So simply use these clear passages as the key, and you will have unlocked the meaning of the obscure passage.

As the Tubingen Lutheran scholars argued in their first exchange of letters with Patriarch Jeremias II:

> Therefore, no better way could ever be found to interpret the Scriptures, other than that Scripture be interpreted by Scripture, that is to say, through itself. For the entire Scripture has been dictated by the one and the same Spirit, who best understands His own will and is best able to state His own meaning.[12]

As promising as this method seems, it soon proved an insufficient solution to the problem of Protestant chaos and division. The point at which this approach disintegrates is in determining which passages are clear and which are obscure.

Those Protestants who believe it is impossible for a Christian to lose his salvation see a number of passages which they maintain

---

[12] Mastrantonis, p. 115.

quite clearly teach their doctrine of eternal security. For example, "For the gifts and callings of God are without repentance" (Romans 11:29), and "My sheep hear my voice, and I know them, and they follow me: and I give unto them eternal life; and they shall never perish, neither shall any man pluck them out of my hand" (John 10:27, 28).

But when such Protestants come across verses which seem to teach salvation can be lost, such as "The righteousness of the righteous shall not deliver him in the day of his transgression" (Ezekiel 33:12), and "He that endureth unto the end shall be saved" (Matthew 10:22; cf. 24:13; Revelation 2:7, 11, 17, 26; 3:5, 12; cf. 21:7), they use their passages that are "clear" to explain away these passages that are "unclear."

Arminians, who believe a man may lose salvation if he turns his back on God, find no obscurity in such warnings. On the contrary, to them they are quite clear!

APPROACH #4: Historical-critical exegesis

Drowning in a sea of subjective opinion and division, Protestants quickly began grasping for any intellectual method with a fig leaf of objectivity. As time went by, and divisions multiplied, science and reason increasingly became the standard by which Protestant theologians hoped to bring about consistency in their biblical interpretations.

This "scientific" approach, which has come to dominate Protestant scholarship, and in this century has even begun to dominate Roman Catholic scholarship, is generally referred to as "historical-critical" exegesis. With the dawn of the so-called "Enlightenment," science seemed to be capable of solving all the world's problems. Thus, Protestant scholarship began applying the philosophy and methodology of the sciences to theology and the Bible.

Since the Enlightenment, Protestant scholars have analyzed every aspect of the Bible: its history, manuscripts, and languages. As if the Holy Scriptures were an archaeological dig, these scholars have sought to analyze each bone and fragment with the best and latest science has to offer. To be fair, some useful knowledge has been produced by this scholarship. But as a means of interpretation, and in its effort to bring unity, it just has not worked.

Like the other approaches, the historical-critical method seeks to understand the Bible while ignoring Church Tradition. It's the same mistake on a pseudo-scientific level.

Though there is no singular Protestant method of exegesis, they all have as their goal to "let the Scripture speak for itself." No one claiming to be Christian could be against what the Scripture would "say" if it were indeed "speaking for itself" through these methods. The problem is that those who appoint themselves as tongues for the Scripture filter it through their own personal assumptions.

While claiming to be objective, they rather interpret the Scriptures according to their own sets of traditions and dogmas, be they fundamentalists or liberal rationalists. If I may loosely borrow a line from Albert Schweitzer, Protestant scholars have looked into the well of history to find the meaning of the Bible, and they have brilliantly written volume upon volume on the subject, but unfortunately they have only seen their own reflections.

Furthermore, one of the most glaring inconsistencies of historical-critical exegesis is its unbiblical character. It soon becomes apparent to the average Protestant freshman Bible Literature student that the Apostles were not very good exegetes—because it is quite clear that they did not follow the methods of critical exegesis. One must conclude either that Protestants understand the Bible better than the Apostles (a claim which, for all its obvious presumptuousness, is made more often than many would imagine), or that the approach Protestants use is fundamentally flawed and at variance with the apostolic understanding of the Scriptures.

Despite all pretensions to the contrary, these methods are far from being neutral tools of science. Modern scholars pride themselves on their ability to analyze critically the assumptions and cultural prejudices of thinkers of previous ages; but in their modern pride, they themselves have been blinded to the way their own assumptions have prejudiced their thinking.

The methods of historical criticism are rooted in naturalistic reductionism, individualism, and relativism. Scientific empiricism is seen as the final court of appeal, despite the fact that empirical methods can address only those things that can be observed or experienced, and thus theology is by definition incapable of being squeezed into the confines of the scope of empiricism. Protestant biblical scholars, failing to recognize the limits of historical-critical methodologies, and filling in the gaps with scholarly schmooze and personal opinion disguised as evidence, have managed to make their work appear as the inevitable conclusions of objective "scientific" inquiry into the Bible.[13] Unfortunately, the inevitable conclusion of applying empirical methods to theological subject matter is that there is not much that we can know about it. Only those questions which their methods can answer are deemed worth asking, and only those parts of the Bible that can survive a full array of skeptical savagery are considered authentic.[14]

Conservative Protestants have happily been much less consistent in their rationalism. They have preserved among themselves a reverence for the Scriptures and a belief in their inspiration. Nevertheless

---

[13] As Thomas Oden observes: "Scripture criticism is more firmly captive today to its modern (naturalistic, narcissistic, individualistic) Zeitgeist than Augustinianism ever was to Platonism or Thomism to Aristotelianism. Trapped in modern prejudices against pre-modern forms of consciousness, reductionistic exegesis has proven to be just as prone to speculation as were the extremist forms of Gnosticism and as uncritical of its own presuppositions as supralapsarian Protestant scholasticism" (Thomas Oden, *Agenda for Theology: After Modernity What?* [Grand Rapids, MI: Zondervan, 1990], p. 111).

[14] Protestant biblical scholars continue to apply the methods of literary analysis that have long ago been abandoned as "fruitless and speculative" in other fields of literary study (Thomas Oden, *The Word of Life,* Systematic Theology: Vol. 2 [New York: Harper & Row, 1989], p. 223).

their approach—even among the most dogged fundamentalists—is still essentially rooted in the same spirit of rationalism as is that of the liberals.

A prime example of this is to be found among dispensational fundamentalists, who hold to an elaborate theory which posits that at various stages in history God has dealt with man according to different "dispensations" (such as the "Adamic dispensation," the "Noahic dispensation," the "Mosaic dispensation," the "Davidic dispensation," and so on). One can see that there is a degree of truth in this theory, but beyond these Old Testament dispensations, they teach that currently we are under a different "dispensation" than were the Christians of the first century. Though miracles continued through the New Testament period, they no longer occur today. In addition to lacking any scriptural basis, this theory allows dispensationalists to affirm the miracles of the Bible, while at the same time allowing them to be empiricists in their everyday life.

Though the discussion of this approach may at first glance seem to be of only academic interest and far removed from the reality of dealing with the average Protestant, in fact even the average piously conservative Protestant layman is not unaffected by this sort of rationalism.

Though conservative Protestants see themselves as being in almost complete opposition to Protestant liberalism, they nonetheless use essentially the same kinds of methods in their study of the Scriptures. And along with these methodologies come their underlying philosophical assumptions. Thus the difference between the liberals and the conservatives is not in reality a difference of basic assumptions, but rather a difference in how far they have taken them to their inherent conclusions.

The great fallacy in this so-called scientific approach to the Scriptures lies in the fallacious application of empiricist assumptions to the study of history, Scripture, and theology. Empirical methods work reasonably well when they are correctly applied to natural sciences, but when they are applied where they cannot possibly work, such as in history (which cannot be repeated or experimented upon), they cannot produce either consistent or accurate results.[15] Scientists have yet to invent a telescope capable of peering into the spirit world, and yet many Protestant scholars assert that in the light of science the idea of the existence of demons or of the devil has been disproven. One searches in vain, however, for the scientific study that has proven this to be the case. Although such empiricists pride themselves on their "openness," they are blinded by their assumptions to such an extent that they cannot see anything that does not fit their vision of reality.

If the methods of empiricism were consistently applied, they would discredit all knowledge (including empiricism), but empiricism is permitted to be inconsistent by those who hold to it "because its ruthless mutilation of human experience lends it such a high reputation for scientific severity, that its prestige overrides the defectiveness of its own foundations."[16]

If Protestant exegesis were truly scientific, as it presents itself to be, its results would show consistency. If its methods were merely unbiased "technologies" (as many view them), then it would not matter who used them; they would work the same way for everyone. But what do we find when we examine the current status of Protestant biblical studies? In the estimation of the "experts" themselves, Protestant biblical scholarship is in a crisis.[17] In fact this crisis is perhaps best illustrated by the admission of a recognized Protestant Old Testament scholar, Gerhard Hasel, that during the 1970s five new Old Testament theologies had been produced, "but not one

---

[15] See Appendix for a discussion of empiricist assumptions in Protestant scholarship.

[16] Rev. Robert T. Osborn, "Faith as Personal Knowledge," *Scottish Journal of Theology* 28 (February, 1975), pp. 101-126.

[17] Gerhard Hasel, *Old Testament Theology: Basic Issues in the Current Debate* (Grand Rapids, MI: Eerdmans Publishing Company, 1982), p. 9.

agrees in approach and method with any of the others."[18]

In fact it is amazing, considering the self-proclaimed high standard of scholarship in Protestant biblical studies, that one can take one's pick of limitless conclusions on almost any issue and find "good scholarship" to back it up. In other words, you can just about come to any conclusion that suits you on a particular day or issue, and you can find a Ph.D. who will advocate it.

This is certainly not science in the same sense as physics or chemistry! What we are dealing with is a field of learning that presents itself as objective science, but which in fact is a pseudo-science, concealing a variety of competing philosophical and theological perspectives. It is pseudo-science because, until scientists develop instruments capable of examining and understanding God, objective scientific theology or biblical interpretation is an impossibility.

This is not to say that there is nothing that is genuinely scholarly or useful in Protestant biblical studies. But no matter how they are camouflaged by the legitimate aspects of historical and linguistic learning, and hidden by the fog machines and mirrors of pseudo-science, we discover in reality that Protestant methods of biblical interpretation are both the product and the servant of Protestant theological and philosophical assumptions.[19]

With subjectivity that surpasses that of the most speculative Freudian psychoanalysts, Protestant scholars selectively choose the "facts" and "evidence" that suit their agenda and then proceed, with their conclusions essentially predetermined by their basic assumptions, to apply their methods to the Holy Scriptures—all the while

---

[18] Ibid., p. 7.

[19] I have discussed liberal Protestantism only to demonstrate the fallacies of "historical" exegesis. An Orthodox Christian is much more likely to be confronted by a conservative fundamentalist or a charismatic, simply because they take their faith seriously enough to seek to convert others to it. Liberal Protestant denominations have their hands full trying to keep their own parishioners, and are not noted for their evangelistic zeal.

thinking themselves to be dispassionate scientists.[20] And since modern universities do not give out Ph.D.'s to those who merely pass on the unadulterated Truth, these scholars seek to outdo each other by coming up with new "creative" theories. This is the very essence of heresy: novelty, arrogant personal opinion, and self-deception.

---

[20] For a more in-depth critique of the excesses of the historical-critical method, see Thomas Oden, *Agenda for Theology: After Modernity What?* (Grand Rapids, MI: Zondervan, 1990), pp. 103-147.

Section II

THE ORTHODOX APPROACH TO HOLY SCRIPTURE

When, by God's mercy, I found the Orthodox Faith, I had no desire to give the methods of Protestant biblical studies a second look. Unfortunately, I have found that Protestant methods and assumptions have managed to infect even some circles within the Orthodox Church. The reason for this is, as stated above, that the Protestant approach to Scripture has been portrayed as "science."

Some in the Orthodox Church feel they do the Church a great favor by introducing this error into our seminaries and parishes. But this is nothing new; this is how heresy has always sought to deceive the faithful.

As Saint Irenaeus said, as he began his attack on the heresies current in his day:

> By means of specious and plausible words, they cunningly allure the simple-minded to inquire into their system; but they nevertheless clumsily destroy them, while they initiate them into their blasphemous opinions.
>
> Error, indeed, is never set forth in its naked deformity, lest, being thus exposed, it should at once be detected. But it is craftily decked out in an attractive dress, so as, by its outward form, to make it appear to the inexperienced (ridiculous as the expression may seem) more true than truth itself.[21]

---

[21] A. Cleveland Coxe, trans., *Ante-Nicene Fathers,* vol. 1, *The Apostolic Fathers with Justin Martyr and Irenaeus* (Grand Rapids, MI: Eerdmans Publishing Company, 1989), p. 315.

Lest any be mistaken or confused, let me be clear: the Orthodox approach to the Scriptures is not based upon "scientific" research into the Holy Scriptures. Its claim to understand the Scriptures does not reside in its possessing superior archaeological data, but rather in its unique relationship with the Author of the Scriptures. The Orthodox Church is the Body of Christ, the pillar and ground of the Truth. The Church is both the means by which God wrote the Scriptures, and the means by which God has preserved the Scriptures. The Orthodox Church understands the Bible as the inspired written and living Tradition which begins with Adam and stretches through time to all its members in the flesh today. That this is true cannot be "proven" in a lab. One must be convinced by the Holy Spirit and experience the life of God in the Church.

The question Protestants will ask at this point is, "Who is to say that the Orthodox Tradition is the correct tradition—or that there even is a correct tradition?"

First, Protestants need to study Church history—century by century, rather than leaping from Acts to the Protestant Reformation. They will find there is only one Church. The Nicene Creed makes this point clearly: "I believe in . . . one Holy, Catholic, and Apostolic Church." This statement, which almost every Protestant denomination still claims to accept as true, was never interpreted historically to refer to some fuzzy, pluralistic, invisible church that could not agree on anything doctrinally.

The councils that canonized the Creed as well as the Scriptures, also anathematized those who were outside the Church, whether they were heretics, such as the Montanists, or schismatics like the Donatists. They did not say, "Well, we can't agree with the Montanists doctrinally, but they are just as much a part of the Church as we are." Rather, despite the fact that many Montanists were sincere and generally "nice" people, they were excluded from the communion of the Church until they returned to the Church's doctrine.[22]

---

[22] To even join in prayer with those outside the Church was, and still is,

Unlike Protestants, who make heroes of those who break away from another group and start their own, the Fathers of the Church considered schism to be among the most damnable sins. As Saint Ignatius of Antioch, a disciple of the Apostle John, warned, "Make no mistake, brethren, no one who follows another into a schism will inherit the Kingdom of God, no one who follows heretical doctrines is on the side of the passion" (Ignatius to the Philadelphians 5:3).

The very reason there arose a Protestant movement was that the Reformers were protesting papal abuses. But prior to the Roman West breaking away from the Orthodox East, these abuses did not exist! Perhaps that is why many modern Protestant theologians have recently begun to take a second look at this first millennium of undivided Christendom. They are beginning to discover the great treasure that the West has lost. And not a few are becoming Orthodox as a result.[23]

Obviously, one of three statements is true: either (1) there is no correct Tradition, the gates of hell did prevail against the Church, and both the Gospels and the Nicene Creed are in error; (2) the true Faith is to be found in papism, with its ever-developing and changing dogmas defined by an infallible "vicar of Christ"; or (3) the Orthodox Church is the one Church founded by Christ, which has faithfully preserved the Apostolic Tradition. The choice for Protestants is clear: relativism, Romanism, or reality!

Because *sola Scriptura* could only yield disunity and argument, most Protestants have long ago given up on the idea of true Christian unity, and have considered it a ridiculous hypothesis that there might

---

forbidden (Canons of the Holy Apostles, canons XLV, LXV; Council of Laodicea canon XXXIII). Thus it is clear that the Church has never accepted any form of doctrinal pluralism or denominationalism.

[23] In fact, a recent three-volume systematic theology, by Thomas Oden, is based on the premise that the "ecumenical consensus" of the first millennium should be normative for theology (see *The Living God: Systematic Theology. Volume One* [New York: Harper & Row, 1987], pp. ix - xiv). If only Oden takes his own methodology all the way, he too will become Orthodox.

be only one Faith. When faced with such strong affirmations concerning the Church, they often react with a mixture of shock and indignation, charging that such attitudes are arrogant and contrary to Christian love. Finding themselves without true unity, they have striven to create a false unity by developing the modern pan-heresy of "ecumenism," in which the only belief to be condemned is that which claims to be the Truth! However, this is not the love of the Church, but humanistic sentimentality.

Love is the essence of the Church. Christ did not come to establish a new school of thought. Rather, He Himself said He came to build His Church, against which the gates of hell would not prevail (Matthew 16:17). This new community of the Church created "an organic unity rather than a mechanical unification of internally divided persons."[24] This unity is only possible through the new life brought by the Holy Spirit, and mystically experienced in the life of the Church.

> Christian faith joins the faithful with Christ and thus it composes one harmonious body from separate individuals. Christ fashions this body by communicating Himself to each member and by supplying to them the Spirit of Grace in an effectual, tangible manner. . . . If the bond with the body of the Church becomes severed then the personality which is thereby isolated and enclosed in its own egoism will be deprived of the beneficial and abundant influence of the Holy Spirit which dwells within the Church.[25]

The Church is one because it is the Body of Christ, and it is an ontological impossibility that it could be divided. The Church is one, even as Christ and the Father are one. Though this concept of unity may seem incredible, it does not seem so to those who have gone

---

[24] The Holy New Martyr Archbishop Ilarion (Troitsky), *Christianity or the Church?* (Jordanville, NY: Holy Trinity Monastery, 1985), p. 11.

[25] Ibid., p. 16.

beyond the concept and entered into its reality. Though this may be one of those "hard sayings" that many Protestants cannot accept, it is a reality in the Church, though it demands from everyone much self-denial, humility, and love.[26]

Our faith in the unity of the Church has two aspects: it is both an historic and a present unity. That is to say, when the Apostles departed this life, they did not depart from the unity of the Church. Saint Paul speaks of "the whole family in heaven and earth" (Ephesians 3:15). It's one family, not two. The departed faithful are as much a part of the Church now as they were when they were present in the flesh.

When we celebrate the Eucharist in any local parish, we do not celebrate it alone, but with the entire Church, both on earth and in heaven. Thus, in the Orthodox Church we are taught not only by those people in the flesh whom God has appointed to teach us, but by all the teachers of the Church in heaven and on earth. We are under the teaching of, for example, Saint John Chrysostom to an even greater degree today than when he was in the flesh. The way this impacts our approach to Scripture is that we do not interpret it privately (2 Peter 1:20), but as a Church. This approach to Scripture was given its classic definition by Saint Vincent of Lerins in the fifth century:

> Here, perhaps, someone may ask: Since the canon of the Scripture is complete and more than sufficient in itself, why is it necessary to add to it the authority of ecclesiastical interpretation? As a matter of fact, [we must answer,] Holy Scripture, because of its depth, is not universally accepted in one and the same sense. The same text is interpreted differently by different people, so that one may almost gain the impression that it can yield as many different meanings as there are men. . . .
> Thus it is because of the great many distortions caused by

---

[26] Ibid., p. 40.

various errors, it is, indeed, necessary that the trend of the interpretation of the prophetic and apostolic writings be directed in accordance with the rule of the ecclesiastical and Catholic meaning.

In the Catholic Church itself, every care should be taken to hold fast to what has been believed everywhere, always, and by all. This is truly and properly 'Catholic,' as indicated by the force and etymology of the name itself, which comprises everything truly universal.

This general rule will be truly applied if we follow the principles of universality, antiquity, and consent. We do so in regard to universality if we confess that faith alone to be true which the entire Church confesses all over the world. [We do so] in regard to antiquity if we in no way deviate from those interpretations which our ancestors and fathers have manifestly proclaimed as inviolable. [We do so] in regard to consent if, in this very antiquity, we adopt the definitions and propositions of all, or almost all, of the Bishops.[27]

This definition of catholicity states very succinctly that which is a deep mystery of the Faith. The question being addressed is essentially, "How can we know what the Apostolic Faith is, when we are confronted with various deviations?" The Church has been confronted with this question since apostolic times, and the greatest defenders of the Faith have grappled with it. The question itself contains the answer—we know deviations because they are deviations. Let me elaborate briefly.

"EVERYWHERE"

By "universality" the Saint is not speaking of simple geography. Obviously, in Saint Vincent's day there were many parts of the globe

---

[27] Saint Vincent of Lerins, trans. Rudolph Morris, *The Fathers of the Church*, Vol. 7 (Washington, D.C.: Catholic University of America Press, 1949), pp. 269-271.

which were pagan, and there were regions in which heresies were dominant. Clearly, when speaking of the Faith "believed everywhere," Saint Vincent is speaking within the context of the Church. Furthermore, "universality" cannot be understood in isolation from the other two aspects of this definition—antiquity and consent.[28]

Taken out of its context, the principle of "universality" would be a circularly based argument indeed. This is why Saint Vincent defines catholicity also in terms of "antiquity" and "consent." Obviously, Saint Vincent assumes we accept the premise that the Christian Faith is the True Faith, that Christ established His Church, and that the teachings of the Apostles are the foundation of that Church. Building on this basic understanding, we further assume the Apostles all taught the same Faith; thus an authentic teaching of the Church would be found throughout the Church, not just in one part of it. When isolated and novel teachings arise, they may be identified by their deviation from the norm within the Church. Having identified them as novel teachings, the Church then casts them aside as alien to herself.

Those who seek to dismiss the apostolic witness of the Orthodox Church will point to such deviant groups and ask, "How can we know which is truly the Apostolic Church? Perhaps it is the Nestorians, the Monophysites, or the papists?" But in each case, one can examine the circumstances surrounding the departure of these groups into heresy and see how the controversies that led to their separation were all initiated by their introduction of a foreign contagion into the body of the Church.[29] The Orthodox Church only reacted, like any

---

[28] Saint Paul appeals to "universality" as the *coup de grace* of his argument for why women should cover their heads in Church (which he begins by appealing to Tradition in 1 Corinthians 11:2): "But if any man seem contentious, we have no such custom and neither do the churches of God" (1 Corinthians 11:16).

[29] Despite the revisionist attempts to downplay the real differences between the Monophysites and the Orthodox, the Council of Chalcedon was called to answer a controversy that was initiated by the Monophysite rejection of the

body with a healthy immune system, to ward off these novel diseases.

"ALWAYS"

In the writings of the Fathers, "innovation" and "novelty" are synonymous with "heresy". The Faith which was "once delivered unto the Saints" (Jude 3) does not change; therefore if something is at variance with what has been believed "always" (since apostolic times) it cannot be the authentic teaching of the Church.

This criterion is also called by Saint Vincent "antiquity." Besides looking at the universality of a doctrine—is it believed everywhere in the Church?—we also consider its age: how old is this doctrine, is it Apostolic?

Orthodox understanding of Christ's two natures. Though the Monophysites argue that they only hold fast to the earlier teachings of Saint Cyril (who often used the term "nature" in a different sense from that which was used by others), the fact of the matter is that Saint Cyril accepted this understanding of the two natures of Christ in his "Agreements" written in A.D. 433:

> With regard to the Evangelical and Apostolic expressions concerning the Lord, we know that men who are skilled in theology make some of them common to the one Person, while they divide others between the two natures, ascribing those that are fitting to God to the Divinity of Christ, and those that are lowly to His Humanity. On reading these sacred utterances of Yours, and finding that we ourselves think along the same lines—for there is one Lord, one Faith, one Baptism, we glorified God the Saviour of all (John Karmiris, *Dogmatic and Creedal Statements of the Orthodox Church,* Vol. 1 [Athens: 1960], p. 154; quoted in "The Non-Chalcedonian Heretics," trans. Bishop Chrysostomos of Etna and novice Patrick [Etna: Center for Traditionalist Orthodox Studies, 1995], p. 11).

On the other hand Timothy Ailouros, a disciple of Dioscorus and a rejecter of Chalcedon, wrote:

> Cyril. . . having excellently articulated the wise proclamation of Orthodoxy, showed himself to be fickle and is to be censured for teaching contrary doctrine: after previously proposing that we should speak of one nature of God the Word, he destroyed the dogma that he had formulated and is caught professing two Natures of Christ (Timothy Ailouros, "Epistles to Kalonymos," Patrologia Graeca, Vol LXXXVI, Col. 276; quoted in "The Non-Chalcedonian Heretics," p. 13).

Saint Paul states this principle very clearly: "Jesus Christ: the same yesterday, and today, and forever. Be not carried about with divers and strange doctrines" (Hebrews 13:8, 9). Since the Person of Christ is unchanged, so the Faith of Christ remains the same.

"AND BY ALL"

Not only must we seek that which is universal and ancient, we must further hold to those teachings which represent the consensus of the Fathers, rather than the isolated views of a given Father or teacher. This is what is meant by "consent," or the Faith believed "by all." Infallibility resides in no individual in the Church save Christ alone, and so there are examples of Fathers who, while generally teaching the Faith accurately, at times taught things which were in error. The difference between these Fathers and the heretics is that the Fathers taught these things in innocence, while heretics teach heresy in opposition to the Church and despite attempts at correction. Even Saint Peter erred, but was corrected by Saint Paul (see Galatians 2). Twice in Revelation, Saint John tells how he worshiped an angel, then was corrected by that angel! Consensus means that we look at the faith commonly held by the Fathers of the Faith.

The Church holds the Scriptures to be infallible, but no individual manuscript is completely free from error. Copyists made minor mistakes when transcribing the Scriptures due to their own human frailties and weaknesses. However, by comparing manuscripts we can isolate these errors, and can see clearly the deviations by comparing them with the consensus of manuscripts.[30] Again, all

---

[30] The approach to textual criticism popular among Protestants for the past century, which has taken an idiosyncratic Egyptian text type (retrieved literally from the ash heap) and has absolutized it as "the earliest and most reliable" text, has been ably criticized by other Protestant scholars. It is another manifestation of the many ills of Protestant biblical scholarship, but is too large a subject to be dealt with adequately here. (See the *Bibliography of The Greek New Testament According to the Majority Text,* eds. Zane C. Hodges and Arthur L. Farstad [Nashville, TN: Thomas Nelson, 1982], pp. 803ff. Particularly, the writings of John William Burgon, Zane C. Hodges, Wilbur Pickering, William Farmer's *The*

of the Fathers were human and at times erred, but these minor deviations are clearly discerned when examined in the light of the consensus of the Fathers.

CONCLUSION

In the Orthodox approach to Scripture, it is the job of the individual not to strive for originality in interpretation, but rather to understand what is already present in the traditions of the Church. We are obliged not to go beyond the boundary set by the Fathers and Creeds of the Church, but to faithfully pass on the Tradition just as we have received it. To do this requires a great deal of study and thought—but even more, if we are to truly understand the Scriptures, we must enter deeply into the mystical life of the Church.

This is why, when Saint Augustine expounds on how one should interpret the Scriptures (*On Christian Doctrine,* Books i-iv), he spends much more time talking about the kind of person the study of the Scripture requires than about the intellectual knowledge he should possess. Such a person:[31]

1) loves God with his whole heart, and is empty of pride;

2) is motivated to seek the knowledge of God's will by faith and reverence, rather than pride or greed;

3) has a heart subdued by piety, a purified mind, dead to the world; neither fears, nor seeks to please men;

4) seeks nothing but knowledge of and union with Christ;

5) hungers and thirsts after righteousness; and

6) is diligently engaged in works of mercy and love.

With such a high standard as this, we should even more humbly lean upon the guidance of those Fathers who have evidenced these

---

Last Twelve Verses of Mark, and Harry Sturz's "The Byzantine Text Type and New Testament Criticism.")

[31] Saint Augustine, "On Christian Doctrine," *A Selected Library of the Nicene and Post-Nicene Fathers,* Series 1, Vol. II, Henry Wace and Philip Schaff, eds. (New York: Christian, 1887-1900), pp. 534-537.

virtues, and not delude ourselves by thinking that we are more capable or clever interpreters of God's Holy Word than they.

But what of the work that has been done by Protestant biblical scholars? To the degree that it helps us understand the history behind the scriptural accounts and the meaning of obscurities, to this degree it is in line with the Tradition and can be used. As Saint Gregory Nazianzen put it when speaking of secular literature: "As we have compounded healthful drugs from certain of the reptiles, so from secular literature we have received principles of enquiry and speculation, while we have rejected their idolatry. . ."[32] Thus if useful knowledge can be derived from even pagan literature, then certainly it can also be found in the better examples of Protestant scholarship. In using them, of course, we must refrain from worshiping the false gods of individualism, modernity, and academic vainglory. We must also recognize the assumptions at work and use only those things that truly shed historical or linguistic light upon the Scriptures. In doing so we will understand the Tradition the more perfectly. But to the degree that Protestant scholarship speculates beyond the canonical texts, and projects foreign ideas upon the Scriptures[33]—to the degree that it disagrees with Holy Tradition, the "always and everywhere and by all" Faith of the Church—it is wrong.

If Protestants should think this arrogant or naive, let them first consider the arrogance and naiveté of those scholars who think they

---

[32] Saint Gregory Nazianzen, "Oration 43, Panegyric on Saint Basil," *Nicene and Post-Nicene Fathers,* Series 2, Vol. VII, pp. 398f.

[33] I am referring here to the increasingly speculative nature of modern Protestant scholarship, in which such scholars often spend their time expounding on their own artificial constructions which they have imposed upon the Scriptures, rather than dealing with the text as it actually is in its canonical shape. For example, you will find scholars describing the theology of a hypothetical source, or discussing the meaning of a parable of Christ which they have "reconstructed," but which bears little or no resemblance to the parable found in the Gospels. For a Protestant critique of some of these excesses in particular, see Brevard Childs' writings, most notably his *Introduction to the Old Testament as Scripture* (Philadelphia: Fortress Press, 1979).

are qualified to override (or more often, totally ignore) two thousand years of Christian teaching. Does the acquisition of a Ph.D. give one greater insight into the mysteries of God than the common wisdom of millions upon millions of faithful believers and the Fathers and Mothers of the Church who faithfully served God and men, who endured horrible tortures and martyrdoms, mockings, and imprisonments, for the Faith? Is Christianity learned only in the comfort of one's study, or also as one carries his cross to be killed on it?

The arrogance lies with those who, without even taking the time to learn what Holy Tradition is, decide they know better—that only now has someone come along who has rightly understood what the Scriptures really mean.

The Holy Scriptures are the summit of the Tradition of the Church. But the greatness of the heights to which the Scriptures ascend is due to the great mountain upon which it rests. Taken from its context within Holy Tradition, the solid rock of Scripture becomes a mere ball of clay, to be molded into whatever shape its handlers wish. It is no honor to the Scriptures to misuse and twist them, even if this is done in the name of exalting their authority.

We must read the Bible; it is God's Holy Word! But to understand its message, let us humbly sit at the feet of the saints who have shown themselves "doers of the Word and not hearers only" (James 1:22), and have been proven by their lives worthy interpreters of the Scriptures. Let us go to those who knew the Apostles, such as Saints Ignatius of Antioch and Polycarp, if we have a question about the writings of the Apostles. Let us inquire of the Church, and not fall into self-deluded arrogance.

Appendix

EMPIRICIST ASSUMPTIONS IN PROTESTANT SCHOLARSHIP

Protestant scholars, both "liberals" and "conservatives," have attempted to apply empirical methodologies to the realm of theology and biblical studies. I am using the term "empiricism" in the broader sense to refer to the rationalistic and materialistic world-view that has long possessed the Western mind, and is continuing to spread throughout the world. Positivist systems of thought (of which empiricism is one) attempt to anchor themselves on some basis of "certain" knowledge. The term "positivism" (first used by Auguste Comte) comes from the French word *positif,* which means "sure," or "certain." Positivist systems are built upon the assumption that some fact or institution is the ultimate basis of knowledge. In Comte's philosophy, experience, or sense-perception, constituted that basis; thus he was the forerunner of modern empiricism. (See S.H. Swinny, "Positivism," *Encyclopaedia of Religion and Ethics,* 1914 ed.; and Wolfhart Pannenburg, *Theology and Philosophy of Science,* trans. Francis McDonagh [Philadelphia: Westminster Press, 1976], p. 29).

Empiricism, strictly speaking, is the belief that all knowledge is based on experience, and that only things which can be established by means of scientific observation can be known with certainty. Hand-in-hand with the methods of observation and experience came the principle of methodological doubt, the prime example of this being the philosophy of René Descartes. Descartes began his discussion of philosophy by showing that everything in the universe can be doubted except one's own existence, and so with the firm basis of this one undoubtable truth ("I think, therefore I am") he sought to build his system of philosophy.

The Reformers at first were content with the assumption that the Bible was the basis of certainty upon which theology and philosophy could rest, but as the humanistic spirit of the Enlightenment gained in ascendancy, Protestant scholars turned their rationalistic methods on the Bible itself—seeking to discover what could be known with certainty from it. Liberal Protestant scholars, having finished this endeavor, are now left only with their own opinions and sentimentality as the basis for whatever faith they have left. "Conservative" Protestants continue to use methodologies immersed in empiricist assumptions, while resisting their ultimate conclusions in a desperate attempt to preserve a meaningful faith in Christ and in biblical inspiration.

One clear example of the fallaciousness of applying empiricist assumptions beyond the realm of the observable is the method such scholars use to determine the reality of past events: the principle of analogy. Since knowledge is based on experience, the way one understands the unfamiliar is by relating it to the familiar. Under the guise of historical analysis, these scholars judge the probability of a supposed past event (e.g. the Resurrection of Jesus) based upon what we know to take place in our experience. Since these historians have never observed anything which they would consider supernatural, they determine that when the Bible speaks of a miraculous event in history, it is merely recounting a myth or a legend. But since, to the empiricist, a miracle entails a violation of a natural law, then there can be no miracles (by definition), because natural laws are determined by our observation of what we experience. Were such an empiricist to be confronted with a modern analogy of a miracle, he would no longer consider it a miracle, because it would no longer constitute a violation of natural law. Thus empiricists do not disprove transcendent reality, or miracles; rather their presuppositions, from the very outset, deny the possibility of such things. (See G. E. Michalson, Jr., "Pannenburg on the Resurrection and Historical Method," *Scottish Journal of Theology* 33 [April, 1980], pp. 345-359.)

About the author:

Deacon John Whiteford is a former Nazarene minister who converted to the Orthodox Faith soon after completing his B.A. in Religion at Southern Nazarene University in Bethany, Oklahoma. He first encountered Orthodoxy as a result of his involvement in the local pro-life movement, which also included Father Anthony Nelson (of St. Benedict's Orthodox Church) and several of his parishioners. After over a year of searching the Scriptures and the writings of the early Church, he was received into the Holy Orthodox Church. Father John currently serves at St. Vladimir's Orthodox Church in Houston, Texas, and is continuing his studies at the New Sarov Pastoral School in Blanco, Texas.

Introductory books
on the Orthodox Church:

THE ORTHODOX CHURCH

By Bishop Kallistos Ware (Published by Penguin)

This classic introductory work on the Orthodox Church has become a worldwide standard in colleges and seminaries. Part One describes the history of the Orthodox Church. Part Two outlines Orthodox doctrine and worship. The final chapter deals with restoring the breaches between East and West.

INTRODUCING THE ORTHODOX CHURCH

By Father Anthony Coniaris (Published by Light & Life)

Fr. Coniaris provides his readers with an invaluable introduction to the beliefs, practices, and patterns of Orthodox Christianity. Written in a popular and easy-to-read style, *Introducing the Orthodox Church* touches all the important bases without sacrificing balance or accuracy.

THE ORTHODOX FAITH (4 volumes)

By Father Thomas Hopko (Published by Orthodox Christian Publication Center)

An introductory handbook on Orthodox faith and life. Volume 1: Doctrine/ Volume 2: Worship/ Volume 3: Bible and Church History/ Volume 4: Spirituality. Presented in brief chapters, this handbook series is excellent for quick reference or study, and provides valuable teaching material for both teens and adults.

ORTHODOX WORSHIP

By Williams & Anstall (Published by Light & Life)

Discusses the living continuity between the worship of Judaism (temple and synagogue worship) and that of the Early Church and the origins of the Orthodox liturgy.

THE ORTHODOX CHURCH: 455 Questions & Answers

By Father Stanley Harakas (Published by Light & Life)

A comprehensive handbook, indexed with easy cross-referencing. Answers 455 questions most asked about the history, doctrine, and practice of the Orthodox Church.

APOSTOLIC SUCCESSION

by Fr. Gregory Rogers (Published by Conciliar Press)

Examines the unbroken apostolic chain linking past to present in the historic Church. Written by a former evangelical pastor whose study of the biblical and historical evidence supporting this very doctrine led him to chrismation and finally ordination in the two-thousand-year-old Orthodox Church.

THE ORTHODOX WAY

By Bishop Kallistos Ware (Published by St. Vladimir's Seminary Press)

An excellent companion to *The Orthodox Church*, this book discusses the spiritual life of the Christian, and sets forth the basic issues of theology, but as a way of life for the follower of Christ.

To request a Conciliar Press catalog, to obtain current pricing or ordering information, or to place a credit card order, please **call Conciliar Press at (800) 967-7377 or (831) 336-5118, or log on to our website: www.conciliarpress.com**